Ultimate Date Night

52 AMAZING DATES FOR BUSY COUPLES

JAY AND LAURA LAFFOON

BroadStreet
PUBLISHING

BroadStreet Publishing® Group, LLC
Savage, Minnesota, USA
BroadStreetPublishing.com

Ultimate Date Night: 52 AMAZING DATES FOR BUSY COUPLES

978-1-4245-6074-5 (faux leather)
978-1-4245-6075-2 (e-book)

Stock or custom editions of BroadStreet Publishing titles may be purchased in bulk for educational, business, ministry, fundraising, or sales promotional use. For information, please email orders@broadstreetpublishing.com.

Literary representation: Jeff Roberts and Kenny Roberts of the Jeff Roberts Agency.

Cover and interior by Garborg Design at GarborgDesign.com

Printed in China

20 21 22 23 24 5 4 3 2 1

Contents

Getting Started

Greetings and welcome to fifty-two memorable and relationship changing dates! The conversations that will come out of these dates will strengthen and grow your relationship. Some of the conversations will be fun, and others will require some deep thinking and reflection. All the conversations will draw you and your significant other closer together.

While some of the dates are seasonal, others can be done anytime of the year, so don't feel you have to walk linearly through the book. Feel free to bounce around.

Once a week, we will give you a detailed description of what kind of date you should go on. Then we will give you a discussion idea to start your conversation in the right direction.

We'll also provide a Scripture verse, journal notes for reflection, a place where you can record each date's highlights, and a prayer to close your time together. We also share some stories of our dating adventures and lessons learned along the way. The KEY at the end of this introduction will give you insight into time, money, and romance levels of each date.

We pray as you use this book it will become a valuable tool to grow and deepen your relationship.

Blessings,

Jay and Laura

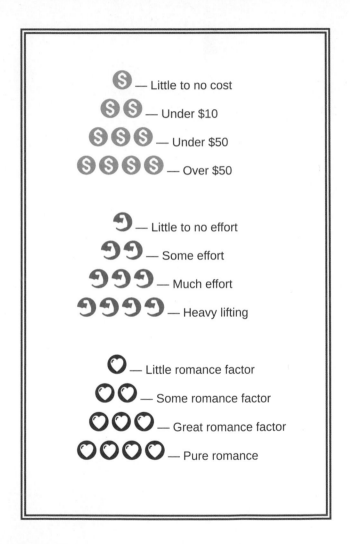

$ — Little to no cost

$ $ — Under $10

$ $ $ — Under $50

$ $ $ $ — Over $50

☾ — Little to no effort

☾ ☾ — Some effort

☾ ☾ ☾ — Much effort

☾ ☾ ☾ ☾ — Heavy lifting

♡ — Little romance factor

♡ ♡ — Some romance factor

♡ ♡ ♡ — Great romance factor

♡ ♡ ♡ ♡ — Pure romance

Picnic under the Stars

It's a picnic in the park at night! Grab a blanket; pack some veggies, fruit, cheese, crackers, and your favorite beverage; and find a secluded place in a local park. If you both like music, pack Bluetooth speakers and play your favorite romantic tunes. After enjoying your snacks, lie on your backs and see if you can name the constellations in the night sky. If you are not lie-on-your-backs kind of people, pack lawn chairs instead.

As you breathe in the beauty of the heavens, share with each other what you would think about as a child staring at the night sky.

CLOSER TOGETHER

Record each of your childhood memories and thoughts you had tonight staring at the stars. Also write down which constellations you identified.

CLOSER TO GOD

God made two great lights—the greater light to govern the day and the lesser light to govern the night. He also made the stars.
GENESIS 1:16

Lord, we acknowledge that you are the Creator of the heavens and the earth. May we always be mindful of that as we walk this earth and be good stewards of your creation.

HIGHLIGHTS OF THE DATE

Date Tip

Make sure there are stars first! Or you might get lost.

We were renting a cabin on a lake in northern Michigan with our friends, Gene and Wendy. Gene brought his boat, and we traveled to the middle of the lake to watch the Fourth of July fireworks from a nearby town. The fireworks lit up the sky in spectacular fashion. However, when the show was over, the night became as black as ink. We couldn't see a thing, *and* we couldn't remember the location of our cabin. We puttered around the lake for over an hour trying to find our cabin.

So when you're planning this date, make sure the stars are out. Share with each other what you see in the stars. Pull up an app on your phone that shows constellations and see if together you can find them.

2

It's Game Night

Locate your favorite board games or card games. If you do not already own what you want to play, go to your local store and purchase it. Prepare your favorite snacks and beverages. Clear off a table and prepare the game for play. Make a night of it even if it means that you play the same game more than once or many different games.

You will most likely have a lot of conversation going on as you compete with one another. Talk about what drives you to win the game and what drives you toward success in life. What does success look like for you?

CLOSER TOGETHER

First and most important, record who won which game! Next, write down what success looks like for you both so that you can come back and remember when you are not feeling so strong and courageous.

CLOSER TO GOD

"Be strong and very courageous. Be careful to obey all the instructions Moses gave you. Do not deviate from them, turning either to the right or to the left. Then you will be successful in everything you do."

JOSHUA 1:7 NLT

Lord God, help us to always be strong and courageous in your strength and power. May we always measure our success by your standards.

HIGHLIGHTS OF THE DATE

Play Time

I (Laura) grew up playing games with my family. My favorite was a game called Aggravation! Jay will tell you it is because I love causing aggravation in others, and he wouldn't be wrong. Our son Torrey and daughter-in-law Shana love to play games. When Shana came into our family, she taught us a card game called Hand and Foot. It causes much aggravation, so I love it.

It is easy to play games when you have a crowd, but when it is just the two of you, it may seem awkward unless you are both die-hard game players. But give it a try! This will go a long way if one of your love languages is quality time. Quality time doesn't have to cost a lot of money, just your time and energy.

Ludus is the Greek word for playful love. Enjoy playing out your love while loving your play.

3

Let's Go on a Treasure Hunt

"Geocaching is a real-world, outdoor treasure hunting game using GPS-enabled devices. Participants navigate to a specific set of GPS coordinates and then attempt to find the geocache (container) hidden at that location." You will most likely want to plan to geocache on a day with good weather. In preparation, download the official Geocaching® app on your smartphone. It is available for all devices. Make yourself an account and geocache away. Happy hunting!

If you really enjoy yourselves, a whole world of geocaching fun exists. If you decide to make it a hobby, you may want to learn the terms for those who love to geocache. You can also upgrade your free account to premium, find more treasures, and log your hunting in the app.

If you were to find buried treasure, what would you do with it?

Closer Together

Write down what you enjoyed about your adventure geocaching.
Record how many treasures you located. You also may want to
record what you would do with found buried treasure.

Closer to God

"The house of my God means much to me. I have much gold and
silver and I give it to the house of my God, together with all I have
already given for the holy house."
1 CHRONICLES 29:3 NLV

Lord, may we always find our treasure in you!

Highlights of the Date

Adventures R Us

Mackinac Island, Michigan, is located in the Straits of Mackinac in Lake Huron. It is a beautiful island that takes you back in time to a bygone era. To get to the island, you must take a ferry boat across Lake Huron from Mackinaw City or St. Ignace. You can explore the island on foot, bike, or horse. No cars are allowed.

Mackinac Island is the first place we geocached. We thought we knew the island very well as we visit it at least three times a year and spend a lot of time walking it. Geocaching allowed us to explore different parts of the island we had never seen. It also caused us to see and observe places and scenery that many people easily overlook.

We found one geocache that is a birdfeeder by a house that we had walked by a thousand times and never noticed. We located another under a boardwalk that we had walked over on every visit to the island. We located a third one next to a cemetery on the island, which was actually a historical site for a feud that took place during the War of 1812. We learned a little bit of history as we searched for that cache, making it even more fun.

Jay and I love doing different activities together. It makes us feel like we are boyfriend and girlfriend again. Dating is more than just spending time together. It is an opportunity to grow as you learn and explore together.

Never stop being your husband's girlfriend.
—Dr. Laura

4

Driveway Date

§ ☽ ♡ ♡ ♡ ♡

This is a great date for those couples who have kids in the house and find little to no time to themselves. Take your favorite beverages and snacks and go out to your car. If you park your car in a garage, back the car out, sit in the backseat, and enjoy some conversation with each other. If you have a truck, take some pillows with you, put a blanket down, and lie down in the truck bed.

Look at your life together. Identify the circumstances (whether it be work, kids, committees, hobbies, etc.) that get in the way of you spending time together on a regular basis. Talk about ways you can prioritize making time together.

CLOSER TOGETHER

Write down the circumstances you identified that get in the way of making your time together a priority. Write down ways you can make this time a priority. Put a date down for your next time together.

CLOSER TO GOD

And let us not neglect our meeting together, as some people do, but encourage one another, especially now that the day of his return is drawing near.

HEBREWS 10:25 NLT

Lord, help us not neglect our relationship. Remind us that this relationship is priority number one only after our relationship with you.

HIGHLIGHTS OF THE DATE

Date Tip

Due to busy schedules, the average married couple spends just four minutes a day alone together.[1]

Our friends Brandise and Trevor have figured out a very practical solution to this problem. They are the couple who gave us "the driveway date." So when you go on your date, ask each other how much time you really spend *alone* together. No screens, no devices, just you two.

---

1 Fact Retriever, "Due to busy schedules, the average married couple spends just four minutes a day alone together," Twitter, February 12, 2017, https://twitter.com/factretriever/status/830927634066321408.

5

Farm Fresh

⑤⑤⑤☾☾♡♡

Find a local farmers market. Take your recyclable bags and head to the market. Decide what would be a good meal to prepare with local veggies and other ingredients. In addition to vegetables, some farmers markets have locally-made soaps, baked goods, honey, and flowers. Take your time perusing all your market has to offer. Get the fresh ingredients to go home and cook a fabulous meal together! Maybe purchase some flowers to adorn your dinner table.

Talk about and plan out the meal you are about to make together. Decide who will do what as you make dinner. Who will take care of the protein? Who will cook the vegetables? Who will get dishes out and arrange the flowers? Who will clean up?

CLOSER TOGETHER

How did you cook the meal? What was it? Consider recording the recipe here. How did you decide who did what as you made dinner? Was there much negotiation or did you both just fall into what you do best?

CLOSER TO GOD

Then God said, "I give you every seed-bearing plant on the face of the whole earth and every tree that has fruit with seed in it. They will be yours for food. And to all the beasts of the earth and all the birds in the sky and all the creatures that move along the ground—everything that has the breath of life in it—I give every green plant for food." And it was so.

GENESIS 1:29–30

Lord, may we be good stewards of all you have given us in food and in our abilities to cook!

HIGHLIGHTS OF THE DATE

One Way

Close your eyes and imagine the juicy goodness of a fresh, red, ripe tomato or the fresh crunch of sweet corn as you bite into it. Fresh fruit and vegetables are hard to beat in flavor and goodness.

Summertime in Michigan, where we live, is a haven of fresh vegetables and fruit of all kinds. You can find roadside stands and farmers markets in almost every town in the state. Wednesdays and Saturdays in our little town will find us at the farmers market. We have our favorite vendors for sweet corn, tomatoes, cucumbers, and whatever else might be in season. We will also make a day of it and go to Traverse City during cherry season or the west side of the state for Red Haven peaches.

More Than Dinner Out

§ § § § ☽ ☽ ☽ ☽ ♡ ♡ ♡

Deciding where to go for a dinner date is always a challenge. You probably both have differing favorite restaurants and types of food you enjoy most. In addition to that, one of you probably always says, "I don't care" when faced with the question, "Where shall we go for dinner?" Tonight, make *her* decide where to go for dinner. No "I don't care" allowed.

Over dinner, discuss little ways you can honor each other. For example, filling a coffee cup in the morning, filling the gas tank when empty, holding a door, letting him go play eighteen holes, letting her go to an evening painting class (or vice versa!).

CLOSER TOGETHER

Write down the little ways you are each going to honor each other in your relationship.

CLOSER TO GOD

Be devoted to one another in love.
Honor one another above yourselves.
ROMANS 12:10

Lord, help us to put the other before ourselves. As we honor each other, may we also honor you.

HIGHLIGHTS OF THE DATE

One Way

I (Laura) am the queen of "I don't care!" It stems from the fact that I am a middle child. We are the peacemakers in the family. According to Dr. Kevin Leman, author of *The Birth Order Book*, middle children make the best spouses because they are used to keeping the peace in a family and are pretty easy going.

No matter the decision, where to eat, what to do next, where to go, I will respond with "I don't care," and usually, I don't. However, this is very frustrating for my type A, driven husband to accept. He has an opinion about everything. Therefore, I have learned to answer the question with what I desire to do. If I really don't care, I tell him that but add, "What about you? Do you have any suggestions?" Then I decide based on his suggestions.

7

Biking with a Purpose

$ $ $ ◐ ◐ ◐ ♡

Having a meal together can be an adventure. Let's work a little for this meal. Find a casual restaurant locally and not too far away. Get out your bikes and ride to the restaurant. If it's five miles or more away, you'll burn off those calories you consume at dinner! If dinner isn't something you want to work for, then bike to a local ice cream shop.

Since talking while biking may be difficult, over dinner (or ice cream), talk about other adventures you can explore in your relationship. Share with each other the blessings that you have in your life. For example, the ability to ride a bike, to eat good food, and to enjoy time together.

CLOSER TOGETHER

Record the new adventures you want to explore as well as the blessings you both see in your lives.

CLOSER TO GOD

May you be blessed by the Lord,
the Maker of heaven and earth.
PSALM 115:15

Lord, we are thankful for the gifts and abilities you have given each of us. Help us not take them for granted.

HIGHLIGHTS OF THE DATE

That's Electric!

While speaking at the Christian Reformed Conference Grounds in Grand Haven, MI, we saw a billboard that read "Rent your electric bicycle here." So we had to check it out. We went in and got the scoop on price and the dos and don'ts and set up a time to rent them later in the week.

It was a blast! We'd never had so much fun on two wheels. The basic premise is that you peddle like a normal bike, but when you wanted to, you could engage a small electric motor that would propel you without pedaling. A simple crank (think motorcycle) on the right handlebar and away you'd go. The harder you cranked, the faster you went. Up to 40 MPH! It was exhilarating. And we didn't have to pedal up any hills. We just let the motor do the work.

8

Planning = Anticipation

💲💲↻🤍🤍

Anticipation is key to any getaway. The fun and romance is more than just the actual getaway. Start the anticipation in the winter or spring before summer vacation season arrives. Take an hour or two and go to your local coffee shop, or even in the comfort of your own home, and plan your summer vacation over a cup of coffee and a favorite treat. Each of you can make a list of the places and activities you would like to go and do on vacation. Get together on one computer and check out places and activities that you can both enjoy. Some websites to use for booking a place would be vrbo.com, homeway.com, and airbnb.com. Use TripAdvisor to find activities around the rental you decide on.

As you begin the planning process, decide on one adventurous activity you can do together that will take you out of your comfort zone.

CLOSER TOGETHER

Record here what adventure you chose and how it stretched you.
Also record other adventures you didn't try yet but want to.

CLOSER TO GOD

May your unfailing love be my comfort,
according to your promise to your servant.
PSALM 119:76

Lord, thank you for your unfailing love that greets us every day.

HIGHLIGHTS OF THE DATE

Why?

In an interview with Michigan's *Big Show*, radio host Michael Patrick Sheils said, "So, Jay and Laura, what you're telling me is that in the area of romance, what was once compelled by infatuation we must now do by conscious choice."

This is why planning is so important. We have to make a conscious choice to build romance into our dating life. So turn back the page and lock down on your calendar your next romantic getaway.

9

Keep the Fire Burning

Something about a fire—whether outdoors in a chiminea, at a campsite, or inside in a fireplace—adds a little romance to any evening. A fire almost always invokes a deep need for s'mores! Head to your grocery store and stock up on marshmallows, chocolate bars, and graham crackers. Build a fire and roast marshmallows to make s'mores. If you can't build a fire, do it over your barbeque grill. If s'mores are all you are looking for, a microwave will do, but then you lose the romance of a real fire.

As you sit around or snuggle in front of your fire, talk about childhood memories of building fires, camping, and eating s'mores. Then talk about the feelings of romance that fire evokes within you. Discuss some new memories you can make around fire and romance.

CLOSER TOGETHER

Write down the new memories you both want to make.

CLOSER TO GOD

Place me like a seal over your heart,
like a seal on your arm;
for love is as strong as death,
its jealousy unyielding as the grave.
It burns like blazing fire,
like a mighty flame.
SONG OF SOLOMON 8:6

Lord, help us keep the fire of love burning in our relationship.

HIGHLIGHTS OF THE DATE

Taking Care

There's one thing about a fire—it has to be tended. Growing up in northern Michigan, I (Jay) lived in a home where we heated with a wood burning stove. All fall my dad and I would cut wood and stack it outside the garage. Daily we would bring in a load that would sit beside the wood stove and supply our heat throughout the day.

The only problem is you can't leave it alone. Every three to four hours, someone would have to put more wood into the stove to keep the heat up. We all took turns because we knew we didn't want to endure a cold Michigan winter night without heat.

So what do you do in your marriage to keep the fire of romance stoked?

10

Getting Away

§§§§))))))♡♡♡♡♡

Getting away, just the two of you, is important to getting ahead in your relationship and keeping the romance alive. Decide on a weekend that is available for you both to get away. Don't tell him what you are planning but make sure his calendar is clear. Find a nice hotel that is affordable for you and book a honeymoon suite. Surprise him with a weekend away in a hotel with no agenda other than being together. No kids, no chores; just the two of you.

In your time together, talk about the importance of getting away from your everyday routine. What are some of the benefits you are experiencing? How can you make this a regular, once a month, once a quarter, or once a year getaway?

CLOSER TOGETHER

Write down the benefits you experienced getting away so you both remember. Put a date down and plan for your next adventure and some possible places to go.

CLOSER TO GOD

Come, my beloved, let us go to the countryside,
let us spend the night in the villages.
SONG OF SONGS 7:11

Thank you, Lord, for our time together. Thank you for the closeness we feel after our alone time and remind us to make this time a priority in the future.

HIGHLIGHTS OF THE DATE

FYI

From the very beginning of our marriage, we have made it a habit to get away on our anniversary. At first, when we were in youth ministry, we'd get away for an afternoon and evening because we couldn't afford a hotel. As time passed and we could put it in the budget, we began to get away for long weekends (mostly to Chicago).

This was our habit until our daughter Grace's senior year of high school. Then we decided we would forgo the trip to Chicago because we had some extra expenses, and it was the last year she would be home.

When we told Grace we were going out for our anniversary dinner, she stopped dead in her tracks and said, "Wait a minute, why aren't you going to Chicago?" She then spent the next ten minutes lecturing us on the fact that we were *not* practicing what we preach. She was *so* disappointed in her parents. We realized at that moment that getting away also models the importance of your relationship to your kids. We haven't missed an anniversary trip since.

Go Fly a Kite

$ 🌙 🌙 🤍 🤍

It's spring, and the winds that come with the changing season are a perfect time to fly a kite!

Preparations:

- ♥ Go to a toy store or hobby shop and purchase a kite.
- ♥ Check the weather to make sure that Saturday afternoon is predicted to be windy.

Part of the fun of this date will be building the kite together. Do it before you leave the house in case you need tools or need to repair an accidental tear or rip. As you leave the house, find a local convenience store and buy one of those slushy drinks you used to get as a kid. Find a local park with lots of space and put your kite flying skills to the test. Take turns flying the kite and recapture the joy of being a kid again.

Talk about the things in your life right now that are robbing you of the joy you know exists inside you.

CLOSER TOGETHER

Write down your "joy stealers" and mark them out with a Sharpie.

CLOSER TO GOD

Bring joy to your servant, Lord,
for I put my trust in you.
PSALM 86:4

God in heaven, we praise you, for you are the giver of joy. As we walk this path together, may we be constantly seeking you and the joy you bring.

HIGHLIGHTS OF THE DATE

Play Time

We were sitting at a table by the beach writing this book. It was a beautiful September day in Myrtle Beach, SC. It was a perfect day to sit and write. The sky was that perfect blue; a few white clouds dotted the sky. The ocean was a bit choppy as the wind was blowing just enough to move the sea grass and the waves.

After a few hours, as evening was just about to hit, a family of four wandered onto the beach and brought out a few kites. We watched as they struggled to get the kites off the sand. They were persistent, though. When the kites finally took flight, they were beautiful. Each one seemed to reflect the person flying it. The young girl's kite was pink and purple. The boy's kite was a dragon. Dad's was red and black, and Mom's was a butterfly. They were having so much fun flying the kites and squealing when they took a nosedive.

Watching the fun they were having as well as putting in a bit of work is the reason we included this date in the book. Dating can be fun for sure, yet it can take a bit of work at times as well. Be persistent and never quit dating each other.

An elderly gentleman spoke wisdom when he said, "Tell the young folks, what you did to get your spouse is what you got to do to keep your spouse." How true!

12

The Spring-Clean Date

$ 🌙 🌙 🌙 🌙 🤍 🤍

Put this one on your calendar early so you both know it's coming.

Spend an entire Saturday spring cleaning the house top to bottom. Work side by side all day long so you can chat about the trivial things going on right now. Tackle the house, room by room, cleaning it together.

- ♥ Dust, including ceiling fans and baseboards
- ♥ Clean windows and screens inside and out
- ♥ Wipe down walls and appliances (including furniture)
- ♥ Vacuum or mop the floors in every room
- ♥ Then move to the garage

Make sure to have some of your favorite music playing in the background as it will brighten your day and make it go faster.

When you're finished, order in a pizza. Over dinner, ask the tough question: Are there things in our relationship that need a "spring cleaning"? For example:

- ♥ Finances
- ♥ Intimate life
- ♥ Expectations of each other
- ♥ Family boundaries
- ♥ Tone of voice with each other

CLOSER TOGETHER

Write down one area in your relationship that needs spring cleaning and create a plan of action to make it better.

CLOSER TO GOD

For your ways are in full view of the Lord,
and he examines all your paths.
PROVERBS 5:21

Lord Jesus, you know that _____ is a trouble spot in our marriage that only you can fix. May we look to you who examines all and seek your help to grow closer together.

Why?

When we moved into our house, it had been owned by a lady who had won the lottery. She and her family mistreated virtually every square foot. But the house had good bones, so we low-balled an offer, and she took it.

Twenty-plus years later, we've put in a lot of sweat equity to fix everything that was wrong with the house. The last project was the master bath. In preparation for the remodel, we spring cleaned our cabinets, finding pills and ointments that were decades old. It was a hoot but also a reminder to "spring clean" our marriage annually.

13

Garage Sale

It's garage sale season and most of the good stuff has been picked over by the pros on Thursday or Friday. So this Saturday, decide to have a morning date competition that culminates with lunch out.

Set the ground rules:

- ♥ You each are looking for a "treasure."
- ♥ You each can only spend one dollar.
- ♥ You will go to four sales before the competition concludes.

Now have some fun! Look in your local paper for locations of garage sales. She picks two, and he picks two. Alternate where you go, with hers coming first. You may find four treasures at 25 cents each, or you may spend your entire dollar on one treasure. The choice is up to you!

Once the competition is complete, declare a winner, who then gets to choose a lunch location. Over lunch, talk about the memories you treasure in your relationship.

CLOSER TOGETHER

Write down the things you indicated you treasured in your relationship.

CLOSER TO GOD

But we have this treasure in jars of clay to show that this all-surpassing power is from God and not from us.

2 CORINTHIANS 4:7

Father God, as we share treasured memories, may we never forget the treasure that we find in your Son Jesus. Amen.

HIGHLIGHTS OF THE DATE

Stuff 'n Things

I'm having a garage sale to get rid of
all the stuff I bought at garage sales!
—Anonymous

Finding real treasure is like finding
a dozen Titleist ProV1's at a garage sale.
—Jay Laffoon

Finding real treasure is like finding
an antique tea pot at a garage sale.
—Laura Laffoon

What we treasure might be totally different, but remember, if it's important to your spouse, it should be important to you.

14

Take a Break

$ $ $ ↺ ♡

It's summer! In most parts of the country, you can arrive at a minor league baseball park in less than two hours. Minor league games are great because you get to see fantastic athletes at drastically reduced prices when compared to a major league game.

The food and beverages are so much cheaper too. It makes for a great, inexpensive date.

During the seventh-inning stretch, ask, "If money were not an issue, where would you want to go on a two-week vacation?"

If you both agree on a destination, then on the drive home have the person who is not driving look into what it would cost to vacation there. Then figure out how much you would have to save and for how long to make your dream vacation come true!

Closer Together

Record your vacation destination and the budget to make it happen.

Closer to God

Trust in the Lord with all your heart
and lean not on your own understanding;
in all your ways submit to him,
and he will make your paths straight.

PROVERBS 3:5–6

God in heaven, we have some big dreams, but you are even bigger. We pray that we would acknowledge you as we plan and that you would make our path straight.

Highlights of the Date

Snafu

We travel for a living, doing about eighty of our Ultimate Date Night shows a year. We get to travel to some beautiful places and some not so beautiful. Travel is either in your blood or it isn't. Some people would just as well stay home as to go somewhere for a vacation.

Vacation is really more about the importance of rest than it is about going somewhere. *Vacation*, as defined by dictionary. com, means "cease work or movement in order to relax, refresh oneself, or recover strength." Rest is good for our physical body as well as our mental body. Rest and refreshment are good for your relational self as well.

We have just finished our winter tour, traveling thirty days out of fifty-five, over twenty-two thousand plane miles and who knows how many road miles! As we traveled to our last show, we looked at each other and agreed we needed to give lots of grace to each other over the weekend because we were exhausted.

We landed in Detroit, anticipating our two-hour drive home to end the tour. We arrived at baggage claim to find that one piece of luggage would not arrive until the following day. Okay, not the best news, but the airline would deliver it, so no worries. I (Laura) began to put away paperwork for the luggage and realized I had left my iPad on the plane. Back to the airline office to see what could be done. A few phone calls and an hour wait, no iPad.

Rest couldn't come soon enough!

15

Footloose

Live music is stirring to the soul and can keep that spark in your relationship, especially if there is dancing involved! More than likely, there's live music somewhere close. Find it and enjoy an evening of music.

As you listen, talk about ways you can add music to your lives, not just in the car on the way to work.

CLOSER TOGETHER

What does music do for each of you? Write down the ways you
can add more music to your life.

CLOSER TO GOD

I will praise God's name in song
and glorify him with thanksgiving.
PSALM 69:30

*Lord, remind us to add music to our lives and that it is good for
worship and thanksgiving.*

HIGHLIGHTS OF THE DATE

Maybe Not

Our son Torrey and his wife Shana moved to Houston so she could finish her final "externship" before becoming a doctor of audiology. They moved in May, and the first chance we had to visit them was August.

They wanted to take us to their favorite restaurant because it had great live music, which it did. What they didn't tell us was that all the tables were *outside* … in Houston … in August! Needless to say, we haven't been back to that restaurant. Torrey and Shana are moving back to Michigan, so we don't have to go back to Houston (and its heat) either.

A Day at the Beach

There is something about water, whether a lake or an ocean, that is soothing to a busy soul. Looking at and enjoying water makes one slow down and breathe. Plan a Saturday drive, just the two of you, to your favorite beach at a favorite lake or the ocean. Pack some beach chairs or blankets. Take along a picnic or stop along the way for some food. Don't forget the sunscreen, a couple of books, and a ball to toss around. Make a day of just slowing down and allowing the water to soothe your soul.

As the day progresses and you begin to slow down and breathe, talk about ways you can slow down without driving to the beach. What are some practical ways you can add quiet to your days?

CLOSER TOGETHER

Record the practical ways you both want to add quiet to your lives.

CLOSER TO GOD

He makes me lie down in green pastures,
he leads me beside quiet waters.
PSALM 23:2

Lord, lead us along the quiet waters and remind us to slow down and breathe on a daily basis.

HIGHLIGHTS OF THE DATE

Date Tip

I (Jay) used to hate the beach. As a kid, I'd get sandy and sweaty and then all salty from the ocean water. But Laura *loves* the beach, and over the years, I've learned to love it too.

How did this occur? I bought a beach chair and an umbrella. Learning to love what your spouse loves does take adaptation. However, the benefits are amazing. I, too, now love to relax and let the sounds of the ocean soothe my soul.

How about you? What adaptations have you made in your marriage that have been for the good?

17

Snuggle Up

$ ☾ ♡ ♡ ♡ ♡

Feel that chill in the air? As summer turns to fall, the night darkness gets longer, and leaves begin to change color, the chillier temps move us indoors. Tonight, after dinner, warm up some apple cider, add a little cinnamon, and snuggle on the couch in front of the fireplace. If you don't have a real fireplace, Netflix has one!

As you snuggle, talk about your love life and some ways you need to add some romance to your life.

CLOSER TOGETHER

Write down one way you are going to add romance in your relationship.

CLOSER TO GOD

Let him kiss me with the kisses of his mouth—
for your love is more delightful than wine.

SONG OF SONGS 1:2

Lord, keep our love for each other strong and our romance creative.

HIGHLIGHTS OF THE DATE

That's Electric!

Snuggling has had its seasons in the Laffoon household. Early in our marriage, I (Jay) couldn't just snuggle. I can admit I had too little self-control to just enjoy the closeness of my wife next to me.

Then as we aged into our thirties, I became a better snuggler. In fact, we would snuggle almost every night as we watched TV.

Now that Laura has started "the change," she says snuggling makes her *hot*. There are nights we can't even hold hands because it makes her way too hot!

18

Doing Something Different

Dinner and a movie, dinner and a movie, dinner and a movie … so boring! Do a progressive date instead. Eat appetizers at one restaurant, your entree at another, finish with dessert at a third. It may take a bit of planning, but it will be fun to experience different restaurants all in one date. Choose your top three favorite restaurants or maybe three you have wanted to try but have not yet.

As you move from restaurant to restaurant, talk about what you liked at the past place and what you liked best about what you ate.

CLOSER TOGETHER

What are some ways you glorified God through your marriage tonight?

So whether you eat or drink or whatever you do,
do it all for the glory of God.
1 CORINTHIANS 10:31

Lord, we pray we bring glory to you in all we say and do.

HIGHLIGHTS OF THE DATE

Date Tip

One of our favorite *Seinfeld* episodes has George, Elaine, and Jerry sitting in the diner with George complaining about how everything he's done in life has been completely the opposite of what he should do.

Elaine notices a woman looking at George and suggests he go introduce himself. George says she'd never be interested in an unemployed balding thirty-something who still lives with his parents.

Jerry tells him to do the opposite and see what she says. George repeats those exact words to the woman, and she replies, "Interesting, tell me more." And they begin to date.

So remember, if what you're doing isn't working, try doing the opposite.

19

Sharing Is Caring

Surprise your wife with a trip to her favorite ice cream place. Tell her you are going to do the ordering. She can just sit back, relax, and enjoy! Order something big enough to share and make sure it is creamy, chocolaty, and has a cherry on top. Get two spoons and dig in.

As you enjoy the ice cream, share how you each could do a better job of loving each other unconditionally.

CLOSER TOGETHER

As you read the following verse, what does it look like in your
relationship?

CLOSER TO GOD

Love is patient, love is kind. It does not envy, it does not boast,
it is not proud. It does not dishonor others, it is not self-seeking,
it is not easily angered, it keeps no record of wrongs. Love does
not delight in evil but rejoices with the truth. It always protects,
always trusts, always hopes, always perseveres.
1 CORINTHIANS 13:4–7

Lord, may we learn to love each other as you love us.

HIGHLIGHTS OF THE DATE

Lovin' Insight

The hardest lesson I've had to learn in my marriage is that my wife is not me. She is herself, emphatically. And her self is a very different self.[2]

—Matt Walsh

I (Jay) used to think that Laura should give and take love the same as me. Why? Well, because this firstborn, type A, driven personality says so! But that isn't so. We need to love our spouse in ways he or she understands. To learn your spouse's love language, go to Dr. Gary Chapman's website: https://www.5lovelanguages.com/. Take the quiz available there.

As you love your spouse, remember, if you were both the same, one of you wouldn't be necessary!

---

2   Matt Walsh, "WALSH: My Marriage Is Not An Equal Partnership, And I Don't Want It To Be," *The Daily Wire*, November 2, 2017, https://www.dailywire.com/news/my-wife-not-my-equal-matt-walsh.

20

Are You Ready for Some Football?

Fall is in the air! Check your local high school football schedule for a home football game. On the night of the game, dress in the school colors and go to the game. During half time, support the sport boosters by treating yourself and your date to a hotdog and a beverage.

This may not seem like a date, but it is. You two are out together, enjoying one another's company, and having fun. What could be better? Hopefully the home team wins!

On the drive to the game or on the way home, share what you look forward to or liked most about the evening. What are some other not-so-date-like dates you could both enjoy?

CLOSER TOGETHER

Write down some other not-so-date-like dates you can do.

CLOSER TO GOD

Dear friend, I pray that you may enjoy good health and that all
may go well with you, even as your soul is getting along well.

3 JOHN 1:2

Lord, in this busy life we live, help us to remember to take some
time to just be together and enjoy each other's company.

HIGHLIGHTS OF THE DATE

Lovin' Insight

I am a dream wife because I love football. Now, just so you know, I didn't call myself a dream wife; Jay did. We were watching Sunday afternoon football, as is our habit when we are home. It can be excruciating as we are Detroit Lions fans, but we love it nevertheless. We were discussing the game, the players, the potential trades coming up, and so on. I made some comments that must have highlighted my football knowledge. Out of the blue, Jay looks at me and says, "You are every man's dream wife!"

I am not tooting my own horn here, but if I want to converse with my husband about hobbies, activities, and things he loves, I need to be knowledgeable. I read up on news articles, follow his teams on Twitter, etc. It isn't rocket science, and it doesn't take a lot of time. I don't have to love football or golf like Jay does, but I do need to ask questions and be able to have a conversation. I want him to converse with me about the hobbies and activities I care about, so I should be willing to do the same for him. As an old saying goes, "What is good for the goose is good for the gander."

Home Is Where the Heart Is

$ $ $ 🌙 🌙 🌙 🤍 🤍 🤍 🤍

Going out to dinner is a great date, every so often. However, you could have the same dinner date on a regular basis and in the comfort of your own home! Go to the grocery store and buy premium steaks, salad ingredients, and yummy bread, and make your own restaurant dinner. There are several videos on YouTube on cooking a great steak, whether on the grill or in a cast iron skillet. Get on Pinterest and find a salad that is more than lettuce, tomatoes, and dressing. Make some dipping oil with garlic, olive oil, and seasonings for that yummy bread. Set the table with nice dinnerware and some candles. Cook together and enjoy the fruits of your labor!

As you cook together, share some other ideas for dinner dates in the comfort of your own home.

CLOSER TOGETHER

Write down other ideas for dinner dates. Find recipes and record
them here as well.

CLOSER TO GOD

You will eat the fruit of your labor;
blessings and prosperity will be yours.
PSALM 128:2

*Lord, working together, whether in the kitchen or around the
house, is enjoyable. Help us to do more of it!*

HIGHLIGHTS OF THE DATE

FYI

We love cooking together so much that we've started a weekly Facebook Live video entitled "Married Flavors." Each week we show busy couples how to make quick and easy meals that are delicious. Our mission is "To help busy couples stay happily married for life!" And what better way to start than with a good meal. To see our videos, go to www.facebook.com/jayandlauralaffoon or to Youtube.com/Jayandlauratv.

22

Care about What He Cares About

$$§ § § ☽ ☽ ♡ ♡$$

Men communicate when side by side enjoying an activity together. The same is true in his relationship with you. Make an effort to take an interest in what he is interested in. Whatever his hobby is—guns, cars, golf, etc.—plan a date to go with him to participate in that hobby. If golf is his passion, take him on a date to play a round. If he is into shooting guns, plan a date at a local shooting range. You get the idea! You will be surprised by what you learn about him and the conversations you will have.

Whatever his hobby is, as you are side by side with him, ask him what it is he likes about his hobby. Make sure you encourage him. Make sure you share with him what you enjoy about doing this together. A word of caution, don't talk too much if it is not appropriate!

CLOSER TOGETHER

Write down other hobbies/activities you can enjoy together.

CLOSER TO GOD

The Lord God said, "It is not good for the man to be alone.
I will make a helper suitable for him."

GENESIS 2:18

Lord, give us the understanding to walk side by side with each other in this journey called life.

HIGHLIGHTS OF THE DATE

Lovin' Insight

When we travel and I (Jay) am driving, I'll often ask Laura to look something up on the internet. One day we were driving to a venue in a rural area where I kept seeing all fashion of barns. I asked Laura to look up why barns are red. She rolled her eyes but looked it up, and here's what she found.

> Hundreds of years ago, many farmers would seal their barns with linseed oil, which is an orange-colored oil derived from the seeds of the flax plant. To this oil, they would add a variety of things, most often milk and lime, but also ferrous oxide, or rust …. It turned the mixture red in color.[3]

While Laura couldn't care less about this, I found it fascinating. I bet the man you love would too.

---

3   *Farmers' Almanac*, as quoted by Robert Clark, "Of Wood and Rust: Old Man Time Marches on in Weathered Barns," *Columbia Metropolitan*, December 2019, https://columbiametro.com/article/of-wood-and-rust/.

23

Fall Decorations

$ $ $ ☽ ☾ ♡ ♡

As fall gets fully underway, this afternoon date is just what the doctor ordered. Find a nearby pumpkin patch or apple orchard or visit your local farmers market for the express purpose of decorating the outside of your house for the season.

Whether it's mums or pumpkins or corn stalks or all of the above, plan out what will go where and get your home ready for Halloween and Thanksgiving.

While you're there, grab a hot apple cider and talk, as you move into the fall season, about the best memories from the summer.

CLOSER TOGETHER

Write down your best memories from the summer.

CLOSER TO GOD

I will remember the deeds of the Lord;
yes, I will remember your miracles of long ago.
PSALM 77:11

Lord, thank you for the seasons you created.

HIGHLIGHTS OF THE DATE

One Way

I (Laura) love the distinct seasons!

Spring flowers.

Summer warmth.

Fall colors.

Winter snow.

I love to decorate our house for each season.

Jay, however, has some rules for decorating. Christmas decorations go up the day after Thanksgiving and have to be down before January 1. Snowmen can stay out during the winter months but must come down March 1. He really doesn't have any rules for spring and summer decorations because if he had his way, those two seasons would last forever. Fall decorations cannot be put out until October 1. No pumpkin or mum buying before then, even if the farmers market has them out.

It doesn't matter the season, when you do something together, it builds your marriage.

24

All about Fun

$ $ $ ◓ ◓ ♡

Today's date is all about the fun. Disc golf is a growing sport in our country, and the good news is you can play most disc golf courses for free. Go to your local sporting goods store, and for your first disc (those over the age of forty would call this a Frisbee), purchase what is known as a mid-range disc for each of you. Simply google "disc golf courses near me" and choose one. Be sure to take water. No one likes dehydration! Enjoy the outdoors while you play eighteen holes. Disc golf generally takes about an hour to play.

While searching for the right course, also look up the rules to educate yourselves on how to play. As you play, reminisce about fun times you have had in your marriage, whether a vacation, special date, or times with friends.

CLOSER TOGETHER

Memories are milestones. Write down memorable moments from today as well as the memories you shared on the course.

CLOSER TO GOD

A happy heart is good medicine and a joyful mind causes healing,
But a broken spirit dries up the bones.
PROVERBS 17:22 AMP

Lord, may the fun and laughter we shared today bring joy and healing to our marriage.

HIGHLIGHTS OF THE DATE

Adventures R Us

We can find fun in just about anything we do.

We were in Florida recently, actually working on this book, and we took some time out to go to our favorite market in the Tampa/St. Petersburg area. I (Laura) grew up vacationing in this area as my grandparents, aunt, and uncle lived here. So as we were headed out to the market, I suggested we try and find my aunt and uncle's house. I had not been there in over thirty years.

I had the street we were looking for and googled it on my GPS and away we went. However, where my GPS took us at first glance didn't seem correct. Jay responded with, "Well, it has been many moons since you have been here and things change." Yes, I knew that, but I remembered a brick road, a curve in the road, and the house sitting on a slight hill. I told Jay my remembrances. He scoffed and replied, "A brick road, really? A hill in Florida, really? Well, let's go on an adventure and see what we can find!"

We drove a while to the other side of the highway, thinking maybe the road I was looking for was actually split and would resume on the other side. And it did! With a bit of detective work, we found the brick road, with a curve in it, and the house still sat atop a slight hill. We were pretty proud of ourselves.

25

Vroom!

Everybody likes that new car smell. The reality though is that we can't all go out and buy a new car just to have that new car smell. Test-driving cars is the answer to obtaining the new car smell. Take an afternoon and hit as many car dealers as you want and drive all the dream cars you can think of!

As you drive, talk about where you are going as a couple. Are you happy with the direction of your marriage, your jobs, your goals? If not, what needs to change?

CLOSER TOGETHER

Write down areas you discussed that needed improvement and the ways you are going to work on improving.

CLOSER TO GOD

The Lord directs the steps of the godly.
He delights in every detail of their lives.
PSALM 37:23 NLT

Lord, help us follow in your steps for our marriage, our jobs, our family, and our lives.

HIGHLIGHTS OF THE DATE

In the Moment

Laura's dream car is a VW convertible Beetle. We were going to Lansing, MI, to test-drive a number of cars as we were in need of a new family car. The first dealership we stopped at was a VW dealer. I (Jay) thought maybe a Jetta would be a good fit for our car needs. We test-drove the Jetta, and it was nice.

Then Laura said, "Could we at least test-drive the new Beetle?" I always thought Beetles were granny cars. After all, they didn't have a turbo-charged engine and a wheelbase that corners on a dime. Then I remembered that we were empty nesters and that we really didn't need a family car. Red with tan interior, we bought it on the spot.

What big purchase have you made spontaneously?

26

fore!

$ $ $ $ ⟲ ⟲ ⟲ ♡

Topgolf is a craze that is sweeping our country! It is like the bowling alleys used to be: food, fun, and friends. Oh, and bowling. Now it is all of that and golf instead of bowling.

Reserve a booth beforehand. You can take your own clubs or use the ones they supply. Once at your booth, order some food and favorite beverages. Pick a Topgolf game to play and take dead aim at the target. Enjoy!

You can't hit a target unless you take dead aim at it. Talk about an issue in your marriage that you need to take dead aim at. Is it money, parenting, intimate life?

CLOSER TOGETHER

Write down a specific target that you need to ask, seek, and knock about.

CLOSER TO GOD

"For everyone who asks receives;
the one who seeks finds;
and to the one who knocks,
the door will be opened."
MATTHEW 7:8

Father, as we seek to stay on target with our marriage, may your Holy Spirit guide us.

HIGHLIGHTS OF THE DATE

Taking Care

I (Laura) am a "math-nostic." I do not believe math exists! Numbers are not my thing. Therefore, early on in our marriage, finances were an issue we had to take dead aim at.

Right out of college, I had a great job and made decent money. However, I was not very good at keeping track of it. Money seemed to fly right out of my hands.

Enter Jay, someone who has every penny he ever earned. Cheap doesn't begin to describe him; actually, he prefers the word *frugal*. When we met, I had bounced fourteen checks totaling over $200 in fees. Now, for those under the age of thirty, a check is something the bank used to give us to pay our bill with, before the age of PayPal and Venmo!

I vividly remember, as we were close to our tenth wedding anniversary, that I had put us in credit card debt but had kept it a secret from Jay. He was talking about taking an anniversary trip to celebrate. I knew we couldn't afford one. It was hard and a lot of tears were shed, but we sat down at the table one night, and I confessed the debt we were in. Amazingly enough, Jay also had a secret. He had been saving for that anniversary trip he wanted us to take. He had saved enough to pay our credit card debt.

Not all conversations are easy, but sometimes they are necessary to strengthen your marriage.

27

Seinfeld?

Put the kids to bed. Fix a variety of snacks and your favorite beverages. Peruse Netflix or Hulu for a sitcom from the past. Snuggling on the couch, listen to the laughter of your spouse. After four or five episodes of your favorite sitcom, press pause and tell each other what you like about the other's smile and laugh.

CLOSER TOGETHER

Make a list of more sitcoms from the past that you would like to binge watch in the future.

CLOSER TO GOD

But may the righteous be glad
and rejoice before God;
may they be happy and joyful.
PSALM 68:3

Lord, help us laugh together more often, and may our hearts be joyful with gratefulness of all you have provided for us.

HIGHLIGHTS OF THE DATE

FYI

While not a sitcom, we recently binge-watched a History Channel series called *The Food That Built America*. It was about titans in the food industry. As Americans moved from the country to the city, demand for food increased and so did the opportunity for entrepreneurs. People like Henry Heinz and his tomato ketchup. The Kellogg brothers and their corn flakes. CW Post and his (stolen from the Kelloggs) Grape Nuts. Innovators like Milton Hershey, who built an entire city around his production facility. And most notably, the McDonald brothers and their relationship with Ray Kroc. These were all innovations that changed American life forever.

What fun we had! Whether *Seinfield*, *Friends*, or the *Great British Baking Show* (one of our personal faves), watching TV together can be a great date night!

28

The Beauty of Art

§§§ⒹⒹ♡♡♡

Google the nearest art museum. Make a day of it. Take your time as you wander through the exhibits created by the artists. Make note of pieces you both find beautiful and those that you differ on. When you are finished wandering, buy a cappuccino and discuss the aspects of your marriage that you both find beautiful.

CLOSER TOGETHER

Document the aspects of your marriage that you both found beautiful and why.

In the beginning God created
the heavens and the earth.
GENESIS 1:1

Father of all creation, you make all things beautiful, and we thank you for the beautiful aspects of our marriage.

HIGHLIGHTS OF THE DATE

One Way

Our Celebrate Your Marriage conferences held every May and October at the Grand Hotel on beautiful Mackinac Island in Michigan are very special events for not only the hundreds of couples who join us each year but for us too. Grand Hotel is over 135 years old and is in and of itself a museum.

Bob Tagatz, Grand Hotel's resident historian, gives marvelous "lectures" on the history of the hotel. We say "lectures" because Bob is really more of an entertainer as he walks people through ages gone by.

Another wonderful treat on the island is The Richard and Jane Manoogian Mackinac Museum. Chock-full of amazing artwork, it's a treat to share their amazing collection of art.

29

Time to Escape

$ $ $ ◑ ◑ ◑ ♡

Escape rooms are popping up all over the country. Some of these live, interactive games are easy and some not so much. Whether solving puzzles or answering clues, all rooms make you work together to escape. Find an escape room nearby and schedule an afternoon of fun. Once you have escaped, grab an ice cream cone and talk about how well you worked together to make the escape.

Then talk about areas in your marriage where you work well together as a team and those areas that need improvement.

CLOSER TOGETHER

Record how well you worked together to escape. What roles did you each play in making the escape? How does this impact your marriage?

CLOSER TO GOD

Though one may be overpowered,
two can defend themselves.
A cord of three strands is not quickly broken.
ECCLESIASTES 4:12

Lord, we thank you that you are the center of our marriage.

HIGHLIGHTS OF THE DATE

Maybe Not

Honesty is the best policy, right? We honestly have never tried an escape room. We have seen other people post their pictures of escaping on Facebook and Instagram. We walked into one with our kids but walked right back out again. It looks fun, but Jay suffers from extreme claustrophobia. He always has to sit on an aisle seat on a plane. An escape room would be a nightmare for him.

Jay is claustrophobic, while I am scared of heights. We were on a cruise, and Jay wanted to do a ropes course that sits high above the ship. I relented and said I would try it. It was the middle of the afternoon, and the ship was docked. I told myself I could do it. Well, the waiting line was over an hour long, and we had a dinner reservation that didn't allow us to wait for the ropes course. We decided to come back after dinner.

After dinner, the circumstances were different. The ship was back at sea. It was now dark. Yes, the course was well lit but still … I strapped in and started up the ladder that would take me to the course. I got to the first challenge and noticed that the next challenge was a gang plank that you walked out over the water! No way was that happening. I turned around and walked back down the ladder.

Jay was disappointed. I pointed out to him that my fear of heights is as real as his claustrophobia. He hasn't asked again to do a high ropes course.

When it comes to dating, we have to be sensitive to each other's personalities, fears, and desires.

30

On a Budget

$ $ $ ☽ ☽ ♡

For this date, set aside a $50 budget and each of you take $10. Find a thrift store and spend the $10 on creating the craziest costume you can for your spouse. Make sure it is something that can be worn in public. When you finish shopping and creating, give your spouse his or her costume. Head home where you must put the costumes on. Use the leftover $30 to go out to eat in your costume.

Over your meal, create a bucket list of crazy things you would like to do as a couple.

CLOSER TOGETHER

Write down your bucket list of crazy things to do.

CLOSER TO GOD

And he said: "Truly I tell you,
unless you change and become like little children,
you will never enter the kingdom of heaven."

MATTHEW 18:3

Lord, may we change and become like children and enjoy some play in our marriage.

HIGHLIGHTS OF THE DATE

That's Electric!

Speaking of crazy things to do, one of our comedy bits in our Ultimate Date Night presentation is a skit we call "bag of dates." These are free or inexpensive dates for you and your spouse. For example, we have a gas pump handle that we stick into the gas tank of our car and drive around. People wave and point at us, and Laura takes their pictures and makes an Instagram story.

Another is to go to the grocery store and read the labels of everyday items. We found a toilet brush that says "Not for use orally"! Someone, somewhere, thought it was a toothbrush?!

Dates don't have to be expensive to be fun!

31

Ahoy, Matey!

$ $ $ $ ☾ ☾ ☾ ♡ ♡ ♡

There is something romantic about water. This date may involve an entire day or weekend. Find a lake near you, or at least within a drivable distance, and rent a boat for the day or a half day. Pack a cooler filled with your favorite eatables and beverages. Pack the sunscreen and plenty of water. Swimsuits and towels are a good idea if you like swimming. Take your time and enjoy the peaceful relaxation of being on the water.

Find a place to anchor. While eating the food you packed, talk about adding peace to your busy life. After you are done eating and talking, snuggle up on a seat and enjoy an afternoon nap.

CLOSER TOGETHER

What steps can you take to add peace to your life?

CLOSER TO GOD

"Peace I leave with you; my peace I give you.
I do not give to you as the world gives.
Do not let your hearts be troubled and do not be afraid."
JOHN 14:27

Author of peace, we ask that your Holy Spirit would give us peace today and everyday.

HIGHLIGHTS OF THE DATE

Adventures R Us

Northern Michigan's Inland Waterway is nearly forty miles long and runs from Pickerel Lake near Petoskey all the way to Cheboygan and into Lake Huron. It's a wonderful trip through four lakes and three rivers. It's a boater's paradise.

One summer, Laura and I thought it would be fun to pack a picnic and rent a boat to take through the Inland Waterway. The only problem was we didn't check the weather forecast and found ourselves midafternoon in a tornado warning. Winds were whipping, waves were crashing, and Laura just kept saying, "Help us, Jesus! Help us, Jesus!"

We made it home alive and with a great story to tell.

32

Bon Appétit

Ⓢ Ⓢ Ⓢ Ⓢ ☾ ☾ ☾ ♡ ♡

Find a cooking class near you. Sign up for some culinary delights. There is something romantic about cooking together. When you take a cooking class, it will not only be fun and romantic, it will also be tasty. Often times you can look at the class calendar and choose what dish(es) you would like to cook. One of the best parts of the class is taking the recipes home and trying them in your own kitchen.

On your way home, talk about the joy of cooking together, what you liked about it, and what you didn't like so much. Often times, one of you will enjoy the preparation side—chopping, measuring, etc.—while one of you will enjoy the actual cooking.

CLOSER TOGETHER

As you look at your experience cooking together, how can the roles you played in the kitchen translate into your marriage?

CLOSER TO GOD

"'Bring the fattened calf and kill it.
Let's have a feast and celebrate.'"
LUKE 15:23

Lord, may we acknowledge the gifts and abilities you have given each of us, and may we use them to bless each other and bring glory to you.

HIGHLIGHTS OF THE DATE

One Way

Cooking together is one of our favorite activities to do together. We did not discover this until we were empty nesters. Our first trip as empty nesters was an anniversary trip to Chicago. We love Chicago at Christmas time. It is not as big and busy as New York City, and we can walk downtown all day, everyday. We have been to Chicago a lot over the years and always try to do something different than just shopping. We have done architectural tours, both walking and by boat. We have done a Christmas lights tour. We visited the Christmas market. We have been to a Cubs game (obviously not for our December anniversary).

This trip we decided to do a cooking class. We had never done one and always wanted to, but living in a small town in Michigan, our options were nil. Sur La Table was located just down the street from our hotel so we figured, why not?

We had a blast! The bonus was we got to eat what we cooked, and we received a discount for shopping in the store. We took advantage and purchased some kitchen tools for back home.

33

Just Drive

$ $ $ 🌙 🌙 🤍 🤍

Take a day, get in the car, and go! No map. No GPS. No agenda. Just go. See where the road takes you and explore what is around you. You will be amazed at what you see, and you may discover places you never knew existed.

As you drive, talk about the feeling of being carefree with no agenda. Turn when you want to turn and stop when you want to stop. After a couple hours, turn on your GPS and head home.

CLOSER TOGETHER

What are some areas in your life and marriage that you need to be more carefree in, no agenda?

But Ruth replied, "Don't urge me to leave you or to turn back from you. Where you go I will go, and where you stay I will stay. Your people will be my people and your God my God."

RUTH 1:16

Father, may we cast our cares upon you and allow your Holy Spirit to guide us.

HIGHLIGHTS OF THE DATE

One Way

Often at our Ultimate Date Nights, the sponsoring church or radio station will do a VIP Q&A with us. Couples come to the show early and get to ask us questions for thirty minutes or so.

To break the ice, we will ask the couples what they like to do on a date. We get the typical "dinner and a movie" response, but one couple said they love to "get lost." One of them drives while the other is blindfolded. Then when they reach the driver's designated destination, they stop, and the blindfolded driver has to find his or her way back home.

Might be a new date for you!

34

Afternoon on the River

$ $ $ 🌙 🌙 🤍 🤍

Find a local canoe livery and reserve a canoe or two-person kayak. Pack a picnic lunch in a waterproof bag or cooler and bring plenty of water to stay hydrated on the river.

Take the first few minutes to get comfortable with the canoe and with each other in the vessel. In other words, find your rhythm as you paddle along. Don't be in a hurry, but instead, enjoy the scenery as you float down the waterway.

After a while, start looking for a place to pull off and have your picnic. Again enjoy the slower pace and maybe even catch a twenty-minute nap! Get back in the canoe and simply float with the current. Sit silently and listen to nature's sounds.

On the ride home, share a favorite moment of the day and what you love about God's creation.

CLOSER TOGETHER

Each of you write down your favorite moment of the day.

CLOSER TO GOD

There is a river whose streams make glad the city of God,
the holy place where the Most High dwells.

PSALM 46:4

*Creator God, we praise you, for you are great and worthy of our
praise. Thank you for a wonderful afternoon in your creation.*

HIGHLIGHTS OF THE DATE

Adventures R Us

Not looking for a pleasant trip down a quiet river?

Noah's Ark Whitewater rafting in Buena Vista, CO, takes hundreds of people every year down the Arkansas River. It's not a peaceful little canoe ride with a picnic. It's high adventure down class III and IV rapids that will have your heart pumping and adrenaline surging! Oh, and afterwards, they'll even throw in a chicken barbeque!

35

Pamper Her

💲💲💲💲🌙🌙🌙🤍🤍

Early in the week preparation:

- ♥ Arrange with her boss for her to get off work a couple of hours early this Friday.

- ♥ Schedule a mani-pedi for her at 4:30 on Friday.

- ♥ Purchase a bath bomb or other bubbling bath soap.

- ♥ Arrange for someone to keep the kids and offer to return the favor.

On Friday, go to her place of work with a pint of her favorite ice cream and two spoons. Walk in confidently with a wink and a nod to her boss, grab her hand, and whisk her out the door. Share the ice cream on the way to the nail salon. Walk her in like a queen and tell her to relax while she is pampered and that you will be back in an hour to pick her up.

During that hour, either prepare one of her favorite dishes or pick up her favorite take out. After picking her up, sit across the table from her over dinner and ask her to tell you about her week. No cell phones, no screens, just eye to eye. When dinner is done, tell her you will pick up her car from work (ask a buddy for help) and will get the kids. All she has to do is go upstairs and take a long, hot bath. Make sure the bath bomb is readily available.

CLOSER TOGETHER

Write down how it made you feel to pamper her.

CLOSER TO GOD

May your fountain be blessed,
and may you rejoice in the wife of your youth.
PROVERBS 5:18

Father, I thank you from the bottom of my heart for the beautiful gift you have given me in _____ (insert her name). I ask that you bless her and keep her at the center of my love.

HIGHLIGHTS OF THE DATE

Lovin' Insight

Love languages play a huge part in understanding your spouse and how he or she gives and receives love. If you have never read Dr. Gary Chapman's book *The Five Love Languages*, order it now. It changed our marriage.

My (Laura's) primary love language is quality time, but my second is gifts. I love to get gifts, and I love to give gifts. Jay speaks both my languages very well. But not always was this the case.

Before we started traveling and speaking together, Jay did most of the traveling and speaking. One particular time, he had been gone for a weekend. On Monday, I thought it would be nice to go to lunch together (quality time). However, Jay had a standing basketball game at lunch on Mondays and Wednesdays. On this particular Monday, I stopped at the game and asked if he would like to go to lunch. He said no. He had just won a game and needed to get back on the court for the next game. I turned around to leave, and apparently, he saw the disappointment on my face because he grabbed his coat and we went to lunch. We now make it a point to do something together once a week.

He speaks my love language of gifts very well! Jay has always been a good gift giver. His giving has evolved over our years of marriage—from homemade love coupons for a hug or cleaning a bathroom early on in our marriage to buying my favorite jewelry now.

36

Short and Sweet

$$\text{\$ \$ ☽ ♡ ♡}$$

One Saturday while out running errands together, pull into an automated car wash, the kind where you are basically in a long tunnel of brushes and towels that dangle over your car.

Pay the attendant, and once your car is fully in the wash, lean in for a long kiss. *Just kissing*! Keep kissing until the dryer cycle is finished.

On your way home, talk about the level of enjoyment that brought even though you both knew it would not lead to anything beyond that. Now determine how often in a week you two should kiss passionately with no other agenda.

CLOSER TOGETHER

Write down your "Weekly Kissing Goal."

CLOSER TO GOD

Your lips drop sweetness as the honeycomb, my bride;
milk and honey are under your tongue.
SONG OF SONGS 4:11

*Giver of all good gifts, thank you for the gift of intimacy a kiss
brings to our relationship.*

HIGHLIGHTS OF THE DATE

Play Time

Okay, just so you know, we practice what we preach. We tried our dating suggestion just the other day.

I (Jay) said to Laura, "We need to try the kissing thing."

She said, "No, there are people here."

I said, "Not once we're in the wash."

It sounds romantic, doesn't it? It all depends on what kind of car you're driving. We were in an SUV with a large center console. Suffice to say, I had to visit my chiropractor after that episode!

37

Pamper Him

Arrange for the kids to go to Grandma's or a friend's house for a sleepover (return the favor next weekend). Ask him if there is a Redbox or Netflix movie he's been wanting to see. If he can't think of one, then rent three you think he'd like and let him choose.

Go to the grocery store and buy preparations for his favorite meal. Before dinner, go with him to the gun range or to play nine holes or to just wander around his favorite outdoor store. Ask questions about his favorite activity like: How did you first get into this? What makes it so special to you?

When you get home, have dinner by candlelight (don't worry about the dishes; do them in the morning). Tell him to pick a movie while you (secretly) go slip into something comfy. (The level of "comfy" is totally up to your comfort zone. Just make sure he knows you're "in" for the evening.)

Don't be surprised if you find him doing last night's dishes in the morning!

CLOSER TOGETHER

Write down how it made you feel to pamper him.

CLOSER TO GOD

How delightful is your love, my sister, my bride!
How much more pleasing is your love than wine,
and the fragrance of your perfume
more than any spice!
SONG OF SONGS 4:10

Father, I thank you from the bottom of my heart for the beautiful gift you have given me in _____ (insert his name). I ask that you bless him and keep him at the center of my love.

HIGHLIGHTS OF THE DATE

Lovin' Insight

When we first read *The Five Love Languages*, Jay decided his primary love language was physical touch. He assumed that this had to be one of his love languages since he enjoys our times of intimacy. His secondary love language is words of affirmation. As a young woman whose spiritual gift is sarcasm and lives in her own personal bubble, I failed miserably at speaking his languages.

After some time, we re-read the book, this time taking the test offered there, and realized Jay's primary love language is acts of service, not physical touch. Whew!

What we realized was that physical touch is not necessarily sex. Physical touch as a love language is someone who loves to hug others, is comfortable sitting close to another. Such people receive love from another through touching. What we came to understand is Jay was not that person. He received love when I did something for him, like clean the house or cook dinner (acts of service). He also received love when I complimented him (words of affirmation). Our intimate life was only a minor part of how he experienced love.

Discovering our real love languages allowed us to understand each other so much better.

38

Ice Cream Parlor

$ ☽ ♡ ♡

Take her to an ice cream parlor where they make real milkshakes and serve them in tall glasses rather than paper. Order her favorite milkshake and two straws.

Sit across the table from each other and share the milkshake. Each of you can only take a sip after telling the other "One thing I love about you is …" Take turns until the milkshake is finished. When you're done, stand up and put a big kiss on her right there in public. Let the world know you love her!

CLOSER TOGETHER

Write down all the things you listed you loved about each other while you shared your shake.

CLOSER TO GOD

I will sing for the one I love.
ISAIAH 5:1

God in heaven, continue to grow our love for each other. May we continually reflect on what we love about each other.

HIGHLIGHTS OF THE DATE

Date Tip

No visit to the Tampa Bay area is complete without going to Mazzaro's Italian Market and Coffee Bar. It is one of a kind. So much more than a market, it's an experience. So those of us who know the ropes start by getting a small gelato.

Now while slowly eating your gelato, you can slowly make your way to the butcher shop, the cheese shop, the wine shop … Oh, and we haven't even made it to the bakery or deli section yet. As you stroll, make a list, and when you are done with your gelato, fill up your cart with food.

Find some of those special places in your area where you can get an experience, not just stuff 'n things. Although, there's nothing wrong with the stuff 'n things.

39

Giving Back

It seems like everyone has clothes that don't fit anymore or are way out of style. So one Saturday, sleep in, fix a brunchy meal, and then head to your clothes closet and chest of drawers.

Spend the next four or five hours (yes, it will take that long) going through your clothes one by one and placing them in three piles.

> Pile 1 – Keep
> Pile 2 – Donate to charity
> Pile 3 – Toss (the clothes no one will wear
>   because they are so tattered)

Put back the clothes you are going to keep, place the toss pile in the trash, and load up the minivan with the clothes for charity.

After you deliver the clothes, find a favorite coffee shop, grab a coffee and something ooey gooey, and talk about how you give back to your community and ways you can do more.

CLOSER TOGETHER

Write down how you give back and the ways you can do more.

CLOSER TO GOD

"Give, and it will be given to you. A good measure, pressed down, shaken together and running over, will be poured into your lap. For with the measure you use, it will be measured to you."

LUKE 6:38

Lord, we can never out give you. May we remember to walk through life with our eyes open to those in need.

HIGHLIGHTS OF THE DATE

Date Tip

For us, we love to give back to the community through Thrivent Action Teams. As members of Thrivent Financial, we each get $250 twice a year ($1,000 between us) that we give to local charities to help them with a project. It's a great way to invest in your community.

Our local Youth for Christ chapter holds a pie auction on the Tuesday before Thanksgiving. Dozens of pies are donated by top bakers in the area and are auctioned off to aid the work of Youth For Christ. Every year, I (Jay) do a $250 Action Team and purchase coffee and ice cream to go with the pies.

You can find a simple way to help a charity with their project. And your efforts can go far. Last year, for example, my Action Team helped YFC raise nearly $30,000. Now that's some good pie!

40

Fancy Date

§ § § § ☽ ☽ ♡ ♡ ♡ ♡

It's time to take it up a notch. Surprise her with a fancy date!

Preparations:

♥ Call and make reservations at a fancy restaurant in town. If you don't have one in your town, find one in a city near you.

♥ Take one of her favorite outfits to the dry cleaners so it's cleaned and pressed for her. Do the same thing for your favorite suit and dress shirt.

♥ The day before your date, tell her what time you are going to pick her up.

On the day of the date, get in your car, drive it around the block, and pull it into the driveway (*not* the garage). Go to the front door and ring the doorbell. When she answers, offer your arm and escort her to the car. Open the car door and close it for her.

Repeat this process in reverse when you get to the restaurant. Use a valet if available.

During dinner, talk about how you felt when you first started dating. What made you fall in love with each other?

When you take her home, pull in the driveway, walk her to the door, give her a kiss, and say you can't wait to do this again. Drive around the block, and while doing so, pull over somewhere safe and call her cell phone just to say again how you enjoyed the evening with her.

You never know what might occur when you pull into the garage and walk into the house!

CLOSER TOGETHER

Write down those things that made you fall in love with each other.

CLOSER TO GOD

Let him kiss me with the kisses of his mouth—
for your love is more delightful than wine.
SONG OF SONGS 1:2

Father, thank you for the gift of love and the chance to fall in love all over again. As we walk with you, may we forever stay in love.

HIGHLIGHTS OF THE DATE

Snafu

I (Jay) did this for Laura for her fortieth birthday. I ended it by booking a couples' massage. I thought we'd be in the same room romantically holding hands while we were being gently massaged.

The night was going great until I pulled up to the spa where we were getting our massages. "What's this? You know I don't like to be touched!" Laura reminded. Oops. I had forgotten that Laura is very particular about her personal space. I apologized profusely but explained I had already paid for it so we should at least give it a try.

When we got into the spa and into our robes, they separated us. Laura went off into one room with a sweet looking twenty-something young woman. They sent me away with Sven, a 6'4" Scandinavian sack of muscles. When we were done, Laura declared she was now a fan of massages. Sven had worked me over to the point I could barely move!

41

The Real Estate Date

It's a Saturday afternoon date that will have you dreaming together.

All over the city, realtors are hosting open houses in homes they have listed for sale. Check the internet for a list of open houses and select three or four to go see. Take your time as you tour the homes and snack on the goodies they have provided.

As you drive to the next location, talk about what you did and didn't like about that home. When you finish your last open house, talk about your dream home.

CLOSER TOGETHER

Write down details about your dream home.

CLOSER TO GOD

Take delight in the Lord,
and he will give you the desires of your heart.
PSALM 37:4

God in heaven, as we dream about our future, may we remember to delight in you first and foremost.

HIGHLIGHTS OF THE DATE

Adventures R Us

Home Town, *House Hunters International*, *Caribbean Life*, and *Beach Life* are some of our favorite shows to watch on TV. HGTV plays a close rival to the Food Network in our house. So when we had an opportunity to tour a *Southern Living* home makeover, we jumped at it! It was a two-hour drive to get there but so worth it.

It was located on the side of a mountain in North Georgia. It was beautiful. It was fun to walk through the house and look at decorating ideas, use of space, and design layout. We made a day of it, stopping for good barbeque for lunch and, of course, a stop at an outlet mall on the way back.

Always look for opportunities to dream together and maybe eat some good food.

42

Take a Hike

Somewhere near you (most likely within an hour drive), there are some beautiful hiking trails through God's creation.

Preparations:

- ♥ Print off a map of the trails.

- ♥ Pack a fun lunch of finger foods like cheese, crackers, salami, grapes, etc.

- ♥ Remember plenty of water.

- ♥ Bring a blanket for the picnic.

Most public trails are loops. In other words, they start and finish at the same location. Pick a loop that will take some time but won't exhaust you. Two to five miles are usually good loops where you can take your time and enjoy the scenery.

Halfway through your hike, look for a shady place to spread your blanket and have your picnic. By bringing finger foods, you will naturally graze and take a more leisurely time through lunch. Over lunch, talk about the path your relationship is on and whether you are happy with the direction you are taking as a couple. You could talk about your career path, your family path, your spiritual path, or any other path you can think needs attention.

CLOSER TOGETHER

Write down which path you discussed and any plans you made to adjust or correct the path.

CLOSER TO GOD

In their hearts humans plan their course,
but the Lord establishes their steps.
PROVERBS 16:9

Lord Jesus, we ask that your Holy Spirit guide our steps as we walk this path together.

HIGHLIGHTS OF THE DATE

Adventures R Us

One of the things we love about our Celebrate Your Marriage Conference at Grand Hotel on Mackinac Island is the chance we have to do some hiking. The island, which is eight miles around and shaped like a turtle shell, is full of wonderful hiking trails and unique destinations like Arch Rock or Sugar Loaf.

One destination we had never been to was The Crack in the Island. It's described as a long crevice that cuts the island in two right down the middle of the turtle shell. It sounded like an adventure. We got there and discovered what is basically a fifty-foot elongated hole. Remember, it's not always about the destination but about the journey and your traveling mate.

43

The Double Date

Preparations:

- ♥ Call up friends and set a date to get together.
- ♥ Agree on a place to meet. (We suggest someplace with more than just food, such as Topgolf, Dave & Busters, or an outdoor shopping/dining complex.)

Plan to spend at least three hours eating dinner and doing something fun together. Keep in mind throughout the evening that many women enjoy conversation and many men enjoy activities (and vice versa), so try to incorporate a good mix of both.

Throughout the evening, reminisce about the memories you share with these good friends.

CLOSER TOGETHER

Write down the qualities you look for in good friends.

CLOSER TO GOD

The righteous choose their friends carefully.
PROVERBS 12:26

Father God, we thank you for the relationships we have built with friends over the years. May we never take for granted the people with whom you surround us.

HIGHLIGHTS OF THE DATE

Date Tip

Going on dates with just the two of you is important and a must in our book, but double dating with another couple or two is just as important. Having friends you both enjoy being with is a great way to build your friendship with your spouse. It is also a great eye-opener to see you two are not so bad as a couple.

We have a few couples that we enjoy hanging around. We have done vacations together. Dinners together. Weddings, graduations, baby showers together.

We have discovered having these couples in our lives adds a richness that we wouldn't have otherwise. We have people whom we walk hard journeys with. People who take care of each other in crisis. People we can laugh at and with.

Find other couples that you can do life with.

44

Belay On!

$ $ $))) ♡

Rock climbing is a really great way to work together and challenge each other to reach beyond comfort zones! You can do this date only one time, or if you really enjoy it, you can join a rock climbing club/gym. Whether you decide to do it once or multiple times, the first time you won't need to purchase any equipment as a gym will most likely have what you need. If you decide to join a club, purchasing your own equipment would probably be a great idea.

As you encourage each other to reach for new heights and climb farther, you will find that with each step you are feeling closer to each other. When you finish climbing, talk about some ways you can encourage each other daily to reach new heights, try new things, and go beyond your comfort zones.

CLOSER TOGETHER

Write down ways each of you needs to be encouraged. Also,
write down ways to encourage the other so he or she hears it.

CLOSER TO GOD

But those who hope in the Lord
will renew their strength.
They will soar on wings like eagles;
they will run and not grow weary,
they will walk and not be faint.

ISAIAH 40:31

Lord, may we use our words and actions to encourage each other.

HIGHLIGHTS OF THE DATE

One Way

Every January we host a marriage cruise called Celebrate Your Marriage at Sea. We travel to different locations and bring along different marriage experts. Years ago Laura committed to doing one "high adventure" excursion with me each year. We've gone parasailing, snorkeling, and climbed Dunn River Fall, to name a few.

One year our cruise ship had a ropes course with a "plank" that stretched out over the ship above the ocean. Sadly, Laura couldn't do it. She is dreadfully afraid of heights and the idea of being over the open water was just too much to handle.

That was a few years ago. This year our "high adventure" excursion was Salsa and Salsa. We learned to make six different kinds of salsa, and we learned to salsa dance. And if you've ever seen me (Jay) dance, you'd know it was "high adventure"!

45

Pickleball

$$\text{⑤ ⑤ ⑤ ☽ ☽ ☽ ♡}$$

Pickleball is gaining popularity as a great sport for fun and fitness. All you need to start is pickleball paddles, balls, and the rules. Some communities have facilities specifically for pickleball, but you could also use a local tennis court. Before trying it out, google the rules as it can be a bit complicated at first. Pickleball is a great low-key game, a mixture between tennis and Ping-Pong, or it can be highly competitive. You choose!

We would suggest for your first time, just play the two of you. As you get more experienced, invite other couples. It can be a great couples date.

After playing, discuss how your marriage can at times be like pickleball—back and forth, back and forth, back and forth. We spend a lot of our time running kids to school and practices, grocery shopping, laundry, dishes, house cleaning, meetings. Then throw going to work in there, and we have no time for each other. What are some ways you can add some consistency to your life? What are some ways you can make time for just the two of you?

CLOSER TOGETHER

Write down the ways you have decided to make time for each other. Schedule it!

CLOSER TO GOD

Yes, my soul, find rest in God;
my hope comes from him.
PSALM 62:5

Lord, may we find rest for our busy lives in you. Remind us to find time for each other.

HIGHLIGHTS OF THE DATE

Play Time

Pickleball is the fastest growing sport you may have never heard of!

According to Wikipedia, "The game started during the summer of 1965 on Bainbridge Island, Washington, at the home of Joel Pritchard, who later served in Congress and as lieutenant governor. He and two of his friends, Bill Bell and Barney McCallum, returned from golf and found their families bored one Saturday afternoon."

We have visited the pickleball museum on Bainbridge Island. We actually stumbled upon it. We didn't even know it existed, much like we discovered pickleball.

We have attempted to play pickleball at our local recreation center with some friends. We are not very good. We bought the equipment. We reserved a court at a time when the rec center is not very busy. It was fun, but I (Laura) think we laughed more than we hit the ball.

Dating is about finding new things to do!

46

Home Improvement

Drive to your local home improvement store. Take a long, slow walk around every department and talk about what you like best in each one. Ask each other:

- ♥ Which stove do you like best?

- ♥ What tile design is your favorite?

- ♥ If you could get any grill, which one would you get?

- ♥ Dream a little with each other.

Now that you've dreamed a bit, have a conversation on your way home about what room of your home you would redecorate first and why you'd choose that room.

CLOSER TOGETHER

Write down your plans for redecorating and put a potential start date (even if it is ten years from now).

CLOSER TO GOD

Unless the Lord builds the house,
the builders labor in vain.
PSALM 127:1

Father, you are the great Creator! Thank you for the chance to reflect you as we dream and create in our relationship.

HIGHLIGHTS OF THE DATE

Snafu

You can pray for Laura. You see, I (Jay) am home improvement impaired. I have to recite righty tighty, lefty loosey when screwing in a lightbulb! I know you're thinking, *Surely, your dad tried to teach you how to fix things around the house*. And you'd be right, but his efforts didn't pay off with me.

Years ago, I noticed my toilet was leaking from the little tube that goes from the floor into the toilet tank. I called my friend Russ who owns a plumbing and heating business. When I explained the situation, he said, "Jay, that's a $5 part at the hardware store. If I send out one of my guys, it's a $60 service call. You can do this!"

I bought the part, shut off the water, and drained the tank just like Russ told me to do. I unscrewed the bad tube and screwed the good tube into the floor. Russ said to make sure the tube was tight (does anyone really know what tight is?). As I was screwing the tube into the toilet tank, I heard the tank crack as a result of me tightening the tube too far. I called Russ. "You know that guy of yours who's gonna cost me $60 for the service call? Have him bring a toilet tank!"

47

Helping Others

Find a local homeless shelter or soup kitchen. Call and arrange a time for the two of you as a couple to volunteer together.

On the day of serving your community, be sure to go into this date with a great attitude of service but also with your heart and mind open to what you might learn. Serve with love in your heart for those you are serving.

Take a check for $50 (which represents the cost of a nice date) and make it out to the homeless shelter or soup kitchen. As you leave, give the check to the person in charge, providing thanks for what he or she does on a daily basis.

On the way home, count your blessings … literally make a list below of the blessings you enjoy.

CLOSER TOGETHER

Our list of blessings:

CLOSER TO GOD

"The King will reply, 'Truly I tell you, whatever you did for one of
the least of these brothers and sisters of mine, you did for me.'"
MATTHEW 25:40

*God in heaven, you have showered us with blessings we do not
deserve. May we spend our days blessing others.*

HIGHLIGHTS OF THE DATE

Taking Care

Every Thanksgiving, a local church in our town hosts Thanksgiving dinner for people who have no family, can't afford food, or just need a place to go on the holiday. Now holidays are big in our family. We had never given up our tradition in order to help someone else, sorry to say.

The local school student leadership groups encourage teenagers to help prepare, serve, decorate, and even cook for the dinner. Teenagers would be at the church at 6 a.m. just to peel potatoes. Our children, as teenagers, helped at this dinner. One Thanksgiving, the kids encouraged us to do it as a family. I (Laura) was reluctant to give up our tradition to do this, but alas, we did.

It was so amazing to see so many people helping others.

Dating isn't always about ourselves. Sometimes it can be about serving others.

48

The Stay-at-Home Date

$ $ $ ☽ ♡ ♡ ♡

Send the kids to Grandma's house or to a friend's house for a sleepover. (If sending to a friend's house, offer to return the favor next weekend.)

Order delivery of a meal *he* has been craving.

Redbox or Netflix a movie *she* really wants to see. Now lock the doors and pull all the blinds. Block all calls except Grandma's or your friend who has the kids.

Eat dinner by candlelight and share with each other three good things that happened to you this week. Watch the movie side by side on the couch like you did when you were dating.

Allow yourselves to be vulnerable together, whether by revealing your innermost thoughts or through physical intimacy, knowing you are completely alone for the night.

CLOSER TOGETHER

Write a three-sentence love note for one another and exchange them. Then write them here.

CLOSER TO GOD

Come away, my beloved,
and be like a gazelle
or like a young stag
on the spice-laden mountains.
SONG OF SONGS 8:14

Lord, thank you for the gift of intimacy. May we never take our love for granted but rather give you praise for the gift of each other.

HIGHLIGHTS OF THE DATE

FYI

We love our job. We love traveling and hosting our Ultimate Date Nights and Celebrate Your Marriage conferences. But while we love our jobs, there are a few things we could do without—schlepping luggage around airports, loading and unloading boxes of books, and eating out.

The stay-at-home date is our favorite because we eat out so much. Let us give you an example. From January 31, 2020, until March 1, 2020, we were home just eight days. Why? It's the month of "love" and the month where Jay gains 20 pounds from eating out so much.

Therefore, we *love* the stay-at-home date! We actually get to share a meal and more in our own home.

49

Christmas Traditions

$\circledS$ ↺ ☽ ♡ ♡

It's the beginning of December, and Christmas is in the air. Call a local retirement home and ask for permission to come and sing carols to the retirees.

Then Friday night, invite some friends to join you and go sing Christmas carols at the predetermined retirement home.

Afterward, invite everyone over for hot chocolate and talk about Christmas traditions from your childhood.

After your friends leave, talk about which childhood tradition you two might want to re-establish in your relationship.

CLOSER TOGETHER

Write down the childhood tradition you wish to reestablish this Christmas.

CLOSER TO GOD

For to us a child is born,
to us a son is given,
and the government will be on his shoulders.
And he will be called
Wonderful Counselor, Mighty God,
Everlasting Father, Prince of Peace.
ISAIAH 9:6

Dear Jesus, may we celebrate your birth and the meaning of Emmanuel, God with us, all year long.

HIGHLIGHTS OF THE DATE

One Way

Tradition: a long-established custom or belief that has been passed on from one generation to another.

Jay and I decided early on that the day after Thanksgiving was not for shopping but rather for decorating for Christmas. On this day we decorate the tree and hang stockings. Remember, I am a gift person, so December is my favorite holiday month. Our entire house is transformed for the Christmas holiday. We make cinnamon rolls to nibble on and hot chocolate to drink as we decorate. We also crank the tunes. Let the decorating begin!

When our son got married, I was sad to think that tradition might come to an end. Much to my surprise, Torrey and Shana made it a point to be at our house on the day after Thanksgiving to decorate that year.

I know it won't always be the tradition it was, but we are ready to make new traditions too.

50

A Family-Focused Date

$ ☽ ♡ ♡

In the middle of winter, it gets dark early. Use this to your advantage!

After dinner, tell the kids you're going to have a family fun night and watch a movie together. When the movie is over, it's time for a bath and bed.

While the kids are settling into a slumber, talk with each other about the "State of the Union" of your family. Discuss topics such as: How are our finances? Have we set proper boundaries with our extended family? Are our kids involved in too many activities and thus effecting our home life? Is our intimate life satisfying?

Once the kids are settled, watch a romantic movie of her choice.

CLOSER TOGETHER

Write down some of the bullet points from your "State of the Union" discussion.

CLOSER TO GOD

The simple believe anything,
but the prudent give thought to their steps.
PROVERBS 14:15

Lord, thank you for our marriage, our family, and all you have given us.

HIGHLIGHTS OF THE DATE

Play Time

A Ping-Pong table. Who would have ever thought a Ping-Pong table would bring a family together, but it sure worked for us.

We have a bonus room over our garage that has served many purposes over the years, from office to library to art room to game room.

Every year we would buy a "family" Christmas gift, and one year, it was a Ping-Pong table. We spent countless hours playing Ping-Pong as a family. What really happened during those times was quality communication with the kiddos. We used the concept of "a family that plays together stays together" to keep communication lines open and have fun in the process. The kids never realized they were being "grilled" by Mom and Dad, but we kept the grilling gentle.

51

The Most Wonderful Time of the Year

Ⓢ Ⓢ Ⓢ Ⓢ ☽ ☽ ☽ ☽ ♡ ♡ ♡ ♡

One of the five languages of love identified by Dr. Gary Chapman in his book *The Five Love Languages* is receiving gifts. If this is one of your wife's languages, then this date is a must! If it isn't one of hers, it will still speak volumes to her. As you Christmas shop, identify a gift that you are going to wrap but not put under the tree. Save it in a special hiding place and make time to give it to her in private. She will be over the moon that you made the effort to make it a special moment.

When you give her the gift, tell her all the ways that she is special to you.

Closer Together

Write down the ways she is special to you and have her do the same for you.

Closer to God

Whoever regards one day as special does so to the Lord. Whoever eats meat does so to the Lord, for they give thanks to God; and whoever abstains does so to the Lord and gives thanks to God.

ROMANS 14:6

Lord, may we treat each other with the specialness we feel for each other.

Highlights of the Date

One Way

When our son was three, we were in full-time ministry together, so supermom here tried to cram all ministry responsibilities into one day so I could be flexible the rest of the week with our child.

Tuesday was my jam-packed day. I would leave the house at 6 a.m. and not return until 10 p.m.—except to pick up fast food for dinner and bring it to Jay and Torrey.

Another fun fact, I hate cleaning bathrooms!

As I have stated earlier in this book, I love gifts and Christmas, and Jay speaks my love language very well. This particular year, Jay gave me the best gifts ever: *Love coupons*! Now normally, love coupons are not on my acceptable gift list. However this year, he nailed it.

While shaking out my stocking on Christmas morning, out floated two love coupons. The first coupon promised that Jay would take care of dinner every Tuesday night for a year! The second love coupon said he would clean the bathrooms for a year!

It was the most wonderful time of the year!

52

Getting the Year Started Right

The end of the year is always a good time to look to the next year, dream about the future, and set goals for the coming year. This date doesn't have to take place on New Year's Eve, but it should happen before January 2! Make some fun appetizers and beverages of your choosing for the evening ahead. Spend tonight discussing your dreams for the new year.

This date inherently has discussion built in, but here are some topics to get you started: vacations in the next year, house renovations to complete, financial goals to achieve by this time next year, healthy lifestyle changes, dating goals for the next year, and more.

CLOSER TOGETHER

Write down your dreams and goals for the new year.

CLOSER TO GOD

Therefore, since we are surrounded by such a great cloud of witnesses, let us throw off everything that hinders and the sin that so easily entangles. And let us run with perseverance the race marked out for us.

HEBREWS 12:1

Lord, may we run the race you have marked out for us in this next year. We commit this year to you.

HIGHLIGHTS OF THE DATE

Date Tip

One of the great tools we have used at this time of year is to choose a "Word for the Year." It really helps to focus you and your spouse on something you really want to make a priority for the year.

The way it works in the Laffoon household is we each choose a word for ourselves, then together we choose a word for our marriage. Words like health, generosity, healing, to name a few, have set a tone for our marriage for the entire year.

One year, it wasn't a word but a phrase. Our ministry had hit a particularly rough patch where we had to lay off staff and take over their responsibilities. What was our word that year? "We'll figure it out!" And we did.

About the Authors

Jay and Laura Laffoon founded Celebrate Ministries, Inc. in 1995 to fulfill their passion for helping couples with comedy-infused marriage events and resources. They celebrate their own marriage of more than thirty years and make their home in Michigan.